INTRODUCTION

The land in Mid-Somerset, known as the Levels or the Plain of Sedgemoor, once belonged to the sea. The region is tranquil with a natural beauty and is drained by the Rivers Parrett and Brue which flow to the Bristol Channel. Many drainage ditches or "rhines" as they are known locally, cross the area, some broad and straight, some narrow and winding. This is willow country. The young shoots from pollarded willow trees were used in wickerwork to satisfy a Victorian passion, and still provide work for local craftspeople.

Between the main roads lies a vast tract of quiet countryside; dairy farming is common and the milk used to make the original Cheddar cheese came from here. Glastonbury, in ancient times an island rising from a vast inland [...] piles in the surrounding marshland. There are great connections with King Arthur, said to be buried here, and the Holy Grail is believed to have been hidden on Glastonbury Tor. There are little stone-built towns in the region and the wool industry thrived here. In the south is the industrial town of Yeovil, famous for its 300 year old glove making industry and Hamdon Hill, where the famous Ham Hill limestone was quarried and used to build many of Somerset's villages and large houses.

The surrounding countryside of green hills is a region of remote villages and small country towns and has its share of impressive houses and visible historical reminders.

CONTENTS

Palladian Bridge in the Stonehead Gardens (Ref: 7734. Picture: D. Pratt)

Bridge over the River Brue (Picture: D. Pratt)

Typeset by Typesetters (Birmingham) Ltd, Smethwick, West Midlands and printed in Great Britain by Redwood Press Ltd, Melksham, Wiltshire for David & Charles plc   Brunel House   Newton Abbot   Devon

Any spot on a Landranger 1/50,000 map can be located by use of a National Grid reference. This is done by noting which vertical line falls to the left of the location and then which horizontal line falls below the location. For example, if we had arranged to meet a friend at the spot height on Rodmead Hill this falls within the one kilometre square labelled 820360.

We next estimate tenths of a square to the right of the vertical grid line, and tenths of a square above the horizontal grid line, to give a standard . six figure grid reference which, in this case, is 822365. You may find it helpful to imagine nine vertical lines and nine horizontal lines in each small square when doing this. On the ground these imaginary lines represent squares of one hundred metres edge (about a hundred and ten old fashioned yards).

Some important guide books, such as those of the National Trust and the Ramblers' Association, now use map references and from these the exact location of anything from a stately home to a farmhouse offering bed and breakfast can be identified.

Here is another example. If we wish to refer to the triangulation pillar on Duncliffe Hill in kilometre square 820220 then, by estimating tenths of a square, we get the full six-figure reference 826226.

This is all that is needed by way of referencing on a single Landranger map although, by adding letters to a reference, one can specify anywhere in Britain, on any modern Ordnance Survey (OS) map, of any scale. If you are interested in doing this, look at the instructions in the margin of the map.

Here is a useful hint for reading and measuring OS map references: "across the plain and up the hill". This will remind you to run your eye horizontally from left to right to get the "Eastings" before you run your eye from bottom to top to get the "Northings". Remember that the hints tell you which way you must run your eyes NOT which way the grid lines run!

Right, what is the six figure OS reference for St Michael's Hill which is in the bottom left hand corner of the map? Next what feature is located by 705439? If you get those two OS references right you can get any OS references right.

(Answers: St Michael's Hill is at 493169. The OS reference 705439 gives the site of the milestone at Leighton.)

Reading a map reference

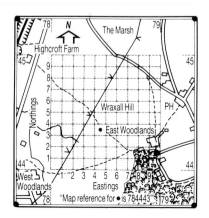

4

Mendip is a fascinating place with much to interest the visitor. Reaching a height in excess of 1000′ on Blackdown, it is a true mountain limestone landscape, its fields enclosed by dry-stone walls. Bleak and windswept in winter when any snowfalls can block the roads for days on end, the area is an officially designated Area of Outstanding Natural Beauty. Throughout the year, it is attractive to explore on foot, horse-back, cycle or by vehicle along its lanes, tracks and wide-bordered roads.

However, to reach those "hidden corners" of Mendip and to get a feel of what roads were like, the inquiring visitor will search out the many "green roads" that still remain to enchant and delight. You need only be a few metres along such an ancient highway, to be totally isolated from the infinitely less appealing modern world of traffic, noise and environmental pollution.

The following green lanes have been selected for their aesthetic or historical appeal. Do not expect them all to be smooth with a green sward! The surface character is very variable and stout walking gear is suggested. Some lanes are rocky, while others can be very muddy, especially if used by farm traffic. Many have public vehicular rights, so don't be surprised to meet the occasional recreational vehicle such as a motorcycle trail-rider or pony and trap. Those seeking solitude and communion with nature, will not be disappointed.

Wells Area – Welsh's Green Lane

(551472). You will find this delightful old lane about one kilometre to the north of the cathedral City of Wells on the Old Bristol Road as it climbs towards the Mendip plateau. Where the road bends sharply left (west), Welsh's Green Lane continues nearly due north and starts as a deep, rocky defile, 20 feet below the surrounding fields, levelling off by old enclosures before climbing again past a "cave dig" and on through the woods alongside a stream to emerge at Ivy Cottage with its thatched roof. The lane is about 1km long.

Old Wells Coach Road (556471) used to be the main road out of Wells to Bristol and was turnpiked at nearby Stoberry Gate. It climbs in a north-westerly direction through woods to level out with good views to the west overlooking Pen Hill Farm and Golledge. Knowing the history of this former main

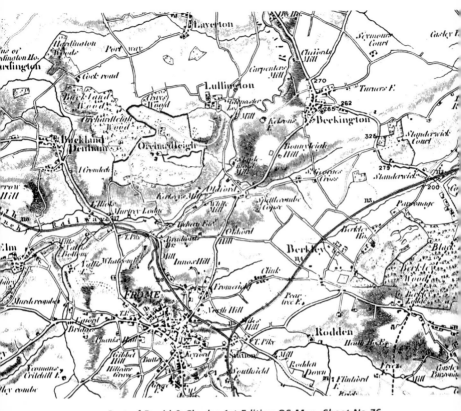

Part of David & Charles 1st Edition OS Map, Sheet No 76

road, now a stony and grass-covered track, will take you back in time as you imagine the stage-coaches and wagons struggling up the steep gradients. If you own a mountain bike, this is an excellent old highway to explore on silent wheels.

West Horrington Road (569476), otherwise known as Biddlecombe, leaves the village of West Horrington to head north towards Pen Hill and the 1000 foot mast that dominates Wells and the skyline for miles around. On the way, by the stream that runs through the woods, you will see the old "Buddle House" which may have been something to do with lead or other former mining activities. West Horrington Road was laid down in 1795 as a carriage road when the "Wastes of Mendip

Forest" were enclosed. It emerges as a headland path in a field at the western end of Haydon Drove, now a tarmac minor road. The correct route exits at a stile, even though it is a definitive bridleway! There is a farm gate a few metres to the east.

The road from Lyatt to King's Castle and Crapnell (560454) – Local historians say that this ancient way was the main road from Wells to London before AD 1200, so you can ignore the 'private road' sign affixed to a tree on the right. This track starts as a green lane past the Wells Golf Club, and skirts King's Castle Wood to emerge on a tarmac minor road north of Dinder, a pleasant route for walking, cycling or horse-riding.

Tanner's Lane (563450) – Although the northern end, (where it

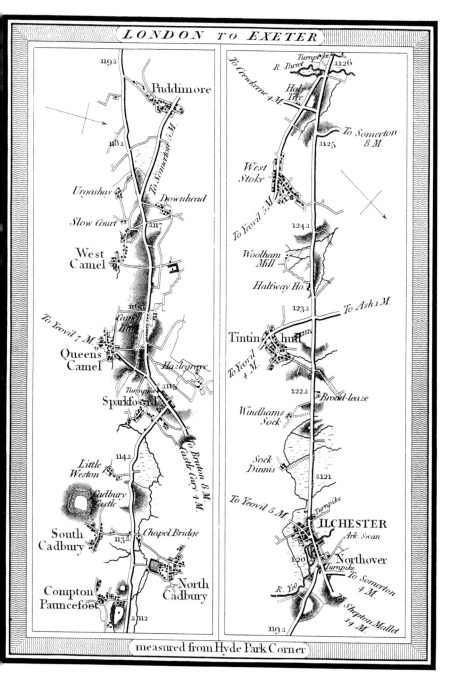

Mogg's map of the London—Exeter road, 1817

joins the Lyatt–King's Castle route) is a headland path, most of Tanner's Lane is a double-bounded green lane. There is a metal stile at the top end just before you enter the field but a sunken line can still be seen, possibly where the old track was once bounded by a hedge.

Priddy area – Eastwater Lane (538505) is an old enclosure carriageway but possesses a bog halfway along it! You need to be determined and not mind getting your feet muddy to negotiate this lane. To the east are the round barrows of Ashen Hill and the Priddy Nine Barrows, while a further half-kilometre to the north are the prehistoric Priddy Circles lying between the B3134 and B3135 motor roads. Swildon's Hole Cave entrance lies about 500 metres to the west of Eastwater and the equally famous Eastwater Cave is just to the east of the southern end of the lane. Please stick to the Rights of Way if visiting these sites.

Dursdon Drove (553487–523496) – This 3km green road runs in a generally east-west direction and was another of the enclosure carriageways of 1795. The central parts are the most attractive because there are farms at each end and the surface has been stoned to provide a firm surface for vehicles. Lying on the top of the Mendip plateau, Dursdon gives ready access to nearby Ebbor Gorge Nature Reserve and is excellent for riding and walking.

Shepton Mallet area. On the

Bolter's Bridge on the road from Sutton to Hornblotton
(Ref: 586334. Picture: G. Thomas)

A361 Frome road, always heavy with lorry traffic from the Mendip quarries, lies the village of Dean. From here, an old highway strikes north towards the main Mendip ridge. Starting at 673442, this delightful lane, Dallimore Lane, was once the site of a turnpike to prevent coal carriers bypassing the main turnpike roads from the Somerset coalfields on their journey south. As you head north along this lane, you will see on your left the remains of a small stone cottage and garden. A local history booklet on the Cranmore area has a photograph taken during the last century of this cottage and the family and children standing outside. How sad it is now a ruin and will disappear one day!

From Dallimore Lane you will see Cranmore Tower, a folly built in 1862 by the Paget family. It is open to the public and commands fine views of the surrounding countryside.

The Roman Foss Way which runs from Charlton turnpike (631432) to near Oakhill is a must for green road enthusiasts. This stretch is 4km long and apart from the occasional deviation, sticks to the route of the Foss. Purists say that the actual Roman agger is just to one side of the existing green lane. It passed close to Beacon Hill (639459), an important meeting point since prehistoric times. Look out for what appears to be a parish boundary stone on the west side of the Foss, just before you start to climb up the side of the Beacon. This stretch of Foss is most picturesque although forestry is obscuring the original skyline and ancient earthworks.

At Edford, (669487) an interesting old coal road is to be seen. Here, the bridge over what was to have been the terminal basin still stands over the remains of the unfinished Somerset & Dorset Canal. Climbing northwestwards to Barlake and Pitcot, "gruffy ground" can be seen over to the left of the lane, the spoil heaps from old mine workings.

Near Blacker's Hill prehistoric hill camp (636500), is Church Lane which drops down to cross Crock's Bottom and then passes Cockhill Farm at 628503. This area of Mendip was once well-populated and various industries occupied the small valley. Remains of cottages lie in the undergrowth. It is a good place to explore on foot.

Strap Lane (628523) runs due north for more than a kilometre to Ston Easton village. Somewhere near here once stood Strap Lane Gate, turnpike of the Shepton Mallet Trust. The lane itself is straight with a stony surface and one can't help wondering at what sort of progress the horse and cart traffic made in earlier times.

Honeywell Lane (596515) at Cutler's Green just to the southeast of Chewton Mendip has an attractive house and garden at the start and continues northwards as a sunken lane between fields before widening out where it meets the B3114. If you are staying in the area – there are some good pubs in the Chewton Mendip locality – you might as well walk or ride Watery Combe (588526) and then Drial's Lane at 597526. There are many less easily identified routes around Mendip but these will provide many hours of healthy pleasure.

TOWNS AND VILLAGES

Central Somerset and the bordering counties of Dorset, Wiltshire and Avon contain a rich variety of towns and villages. Coal mining towns of the industrial revolution, sheep market towns from the heyday of the wool trade, important monastic foundations, all have mellowed to become part of the heritage of this varied landscape.

Radstock (690550) and Midsomer Norton (663541) do not have the appearance of mining towns. They lack the dark austerity of more northern coal towns, giving more the impression of country markets. In the early days of the industrialisation of Britain they were at the heart of an industry supplying the factories of Bristol and the surrounding area. Today the coal mines are museum pieces. The last pit closed in 1973. The twin towns have reverted to their old role as large villages in a basically rural community.

Chewton Mendip (596532), at the source of the River Chew, was

Vicars Close, Wells

once a lead mining village. The Romans came to the Mendip Hills to mine for lead. In AD 901 King Alfred mentioned the village in his will. The grey stone cottages lead to the splendid church of St Mary Magdalene.

Wells (551458) is Britain's smallest city. It is a small market town around a magnificent cathedral. Water washes the gutters of the busy streets, while quiet corners contain architectural delights. The 14th century Vicars Close is thought to be the oldest complete and inhabited street in Europe. The Cathedral Close is lined with ancient buildings, while its gateways are treasures worth discovering. Find Penniless Porch, or the restaurant built over a gateway.

Shepton Mallet (620436) was the "sheep town" corrupted to "shepton" in its name, a satellite of the monastery at Glastonbury. In the Middle Ages the town was famous for cloth and stockings. Many fine houses remain from this period of prosperity. The 17th century terrace in Great Ostry should not be missed. Today Shepton Mallet manufacturers cider, cheese and Babycham, but is best known as the home of the annual Royal Bath and West Agricultural Show.

Glastonbury Tor (512386) dominates the Somerset landscape for dozens of miles around. It draws the traveller like a magnet, just as, so legend declares, it drew Joseph and his fellow travellers, when they came to Britain after the Crucifixion. The story, well known in the Middle Ages, of the island of Avalon (Glastonbury) settled by Joseph when his staff, stuck in the ground while he was at prayer, sprouted and blossomed

on Christmas Day, still has supporters. The Glastonbury thorn still blossoms in mid-winter.

The most precious of Joseph's relics escapes detection. He is said to have brought with him the chalice used for wine at the Last Supper. This was the Holy Grail, so much sought after in the second of Glastonbury's great legends. King Arthur's Knights of the Round Table searched far and wide for the Holy Grail. King Arthur's tomb was found at Glastonbury Abbey after a fire in 1184.

The ruins of one of the wealthiest Abbeys in Britain spread across several acres of green. The Abbey Barn is the centre-piece of the Somerset Rural Life Exhibitions. The George and Pilgrim Inn has served travellers for over five hundred years from behind its elaborate ecclesiastical façade.

Sherborne (638165) was known to the Romans, but was most important in Saxon times. In AD 705 it was made the Cathedral City of Wessex with St Aldehelm as its first bishop. King Alfred the Great attended the Cathedral school. The great Abbey Church was

Mary Rand's world record long jump recorded in her home city of Wells (Picture: I. Thompson)

Croquet players on the Bishop's Palace lawn, Wells

begun in AD 998 when a Benedictine monastery was established here. The bishopric moved to Salisbury, the Abbey was dissolved by Henry VIII, the Norman castle was largely destroyed in the Civil War, but Sherborne still remains an architectural treasure house. The other Sherborne Castle is a mansion, built in 1594 by Sir Walter Raleigh.

Shaftesbury (862229) is the most famous town on a hill. The view down the cobbled Gold Hill to the green fields beyond is known throughout the land. King Alfred built a town and a great nunnery here. The Normans added a castle. The town faded in the 18th century, but is quietly prosperous again today.

Bruton (685346) was another royal burgh created by the Saxon kings of Wessex. It is a picturesque little town, with antique shops and Georgian houses. See the 15th century packhorse bridge, the church with two towers, the priory dovecote and the Jacobean almshouses of Sexey's Hospital.

Warminster (874451) is set against a background of wooded downs. It is a town of small Georgian houses and mullion-windowed cottages. See Vicarage Street and Silver Street in particular. The Bath Arms and the Old Bell are good 18th century inns. St Lawrence's Church has a 15th century tower.

Nunney (738457) was described as the perfect village, having "everything that the heart could desire to make it both lovely and interesting". It has many 17th and

18th century houses built in the local stone, a partly ruined castle, an inn which tries to dominate by spanning the main street with its sign, and a 13th and 14th century church.

Pilton (589406) is set in a hollow in the hills, where the great tythe barn looks towards the Abbey at Glastonbury to which it sent its produce.

Croscombe (591444) fills its narrow valley with stone and pantiled cottages, leading to the Old Manor House which dates from the early Tudor period. Water mills drove the town's woollen industry in the Middle Ages. The 14th century cross still stands at the village centre, despite attempts in the 18th century to remove it.

South Cadbury's yellow stonework (631256) sets off its many charming houses. The 18th century rectory faces the church gate. The old school is nearby. Castle Farm has a thatched roof and mullioned windows.

Eld Bridge at Bruton (Ref: 6835. Picture: D. Pratt)

PLACES NAMES

The earliest layer of names on English maps dates from the arrival of the Celts about three thousand years ago. These names are more common in the North and West. Then, after the Roman occupation, it was the coming of the Angles and Saxons (5th to 7th centuries) which provided the chief source of place-names. Finally a layer of Scandinavian names was given to parts of North and East England by the Danish conquests (9th century) and the raids of the Norsemen (10th century).

Yeovil (550160) takes its name from the *River Yeo* on which it stands. The *vil* ending of the name does not come from *ville*, as one might think, but is of 9th century origin when both town and river bore the name *Gifl*. The name *Yeo* is Britonic and it means "forked river". *Frome* (780480) is similarly named from its river and once again the origin of the name is pre-English. It means "fair river".

Glastonbury (500390) is the "fortified place at the woad garden", *Mere* (815325) is Old English

◄ *The George and Pilgrim's Inn at Glastonbury (Picture: I. Thompson)*

The Market Place is the Private Property of the Lord of the Manor and he requests that you will kindly limit your parking to 2 Hours.

Parking notice at Nunney

Ashley House and Mendip stone cottages at Croscombe
(Ref: 5944. Picture: I. Thompson)

mere meaning "lake", *Sherborne* (640170) comes from old English *scir* meaning "bright" or "pure" and *burna* meaning "stream". *Gillingham* (805270) is the *ham* or "homestead" of the *ingas* or "people" of the local headman Gylla.

The recognition of the different elements of an English place-name is an essential part of place-name analysis although absolute confirmation will usually rest upon the existence of old documentary records such as those in the Domesday Book.

Shepton Mallet (620440) is an example of a two-part name which adds a Norman overlord's family name to a pre-existing place-name. In this case the Old English *sceap-tun* or "sheep farm" was held by the Norman, Robert Malet. Similarly *Charlton Mackrell* (530290) and *Charlton Adam* (538288) combine *ceorl-tun*, the "farm of the free peasants" with the names of the Makerel and fitz Adam families respectively.

Henstridge (723197) is the "ridge where the stallions were kept", from the Old English *hengest* or "stallion". *Binegar* (620492) comes from *bean-hangra*, the "slope where the beans were grown". *Zeals* (780315) is "willow wood", *Bruton* (680350) is the "farm on the River Brue" and *Evercreech* (647390) combines Old English *eofor* meaning "boar" with an older Britonic name *cruc* which means "hill".

16

CANALS AND RIVERS

Although there are no navigable waterways shown on this map, this was not always the case. The Romans established an island port on the Yeo at Ilchester, but it is now many centuries since the town saw any boat at all arrive for trade. Roads not water have formed the most important links, and there is a fine, narrow, high-arched packhorse bridge across the river (500234). There was, however, a canal that flourished briefly that joined Ilchester to the River Parrett, seven miles away to the east. Another canal which has also left few traces was the Glastonbury which again ran east to connect with the River Brue. One can find the faint traces of this waterway by the site of the original basin at the end of Dyehouse Lane (492391).

The other rivers that appear on the map have had their influence on developments in the region, in very different ways. The more important is as sources of power to turn the water wheels of early industry, particularly those of the woollen mills centred on Frome. Rivers can be dammed to form mill ponds or stopped simply to create artificial lakes to enhance the landscape in great estates such as Stourhead (7734) and Longleat (8143). If they do nothing else, the rivers that water the region add to its natural beauty, providing popular picnic spots such as Five Bridges (758215) and riverside walks such as that along the Yeo at Yeovilton (5422).

There was one major project planned for the region, the Dorset and Somerset Canal, which was to join the Stour – the river that appears at 785150 – to the Kennet and Avon Canal to the north of the area. Work began on the central section, based in Frome, in 1796 and it can still be traced in the town, notably as a masonry embankment (771495). Work began on a flight of six "Machine or Balance Locks" which were boat lifts working on a counter-balance principle at Barrow Hill (748500) and the earthworks can still be seen, but by then cash had run out and the canal was never completed.

The David & Charles Britain series is an exciting range of books covering, The Lake District, The Peak District, The Northumbrian Uplands, The Pembrokeshire Coast National Park, and Snowdonia. There are several others planned.

Each volume – written out of deep personal knowledge of the area – provides a thorough background and guide to archaeology, natural history, the development of the landscape, and architectural styles. Each book is at least 200 pages, hardback and illustrated in colour. Buy them from your bookshop or write to us at Brunel House, Newton Abbot, Devon TQ12 4PU.

CASTLES, CHURCHES, HALLS

South Cadbury (628252) is one of the few hill forts that have been thoroughly excavated by expert archaeologists. Professor Alcock's work between 1966 and 1970 revealed an 18 acre site with the most elaborate defences in Somerset. He found that the occupation of the site went back to 3300 BC.

The four encircling Iron Age banks and ditches were modified or rebuilt at least five times. He found evidence of a Celtic smithy and a Romano-Celtic temple. In the south west gateway he found the dismembered remains of thirty

men, women and children, massacred when the Romans captured South Cadbury during their conquest of Britain.

About AD 500 the site was refortified and had a large timber hall with evidence of a flourishing community at the time associated with King Arthur. It is easy to see why South Cadbury has been associated with Arthur's Camelot in legends which can be traced back at least to the Middle Ages.

South Cadbury saw one last Museum including an exhibition of agricultural implements and a

Glastonbury Tor (Ref: 5183)

wheelwright's shop. The Tribunal was the Abbey's Court House, built in 1400. This, too, is now a museum.

Sherborne's abbey (638166)
perhaps fared better. The abbey church survives as the parish church. It includes Saxon, Norman and Early English work but is predominantly 15th century. A notable feature is the fan vaulting of the nave and choir. A museum of local history is housed in what was the abbey gatehouse. The fascinating structure near the museum was built as the monks' wash house. The almshouses in the town were founded in 1437. Sherborne School occupies the Abbot's Hall, the Abbot's lodgings and the abbey kitchens.

Nunney's Church of All Saints (738457) dates from the 13th century, with 14th century transepts. The wagon roof, the tower, south porch and wooden chancel screen were built about 1525. Among the many monuments within the church is one from 1390, depicting Sir John Poulet and his wife Constance.

The spire of St Mary the Virgin, Croscombe (591444), is the finest in Somerset. It was taken down and rebuilt in 1936 after being struck by lightning. The interior contains much Jacobean woodwork. The superb pulpit was a gift of Bishop Lake in 1616.

The entire village of Chewton
Mendip is dominated by the 126-foot tower of St Mary Magdalene (597532). The tower was built by Carthusian monks who established

Bishops Palace, Wells (Ref: 5524)

a priory here in 1420 and covered it with beautiful carving. Many other treasures are to be found inside the church.

Bruton's church (686346) has two towers. The first dates from the 15th century, while the second larger tower was built about a hundred years later. The chancel was furnished and decorated in the 1740s.

Wells Cathedral (551458) was begun in 1176 to replace the minster which had stood in what is now the Market Square since 700 AD. The Bishop of Bath moved his headquarters to the new cathedral at Wells. The West front, containing some 400 statues, suffered when the city was taken by the Roundheads during the Civil War. A contemporary account states "On Saturday 7 April, 1643, the Parliamentary troopers broke down divers pictures and statues in the church and in the Lady Chapel." Fortunately, what remains is still magnificent. The great arches were added below the central tower in 1350 to prevent it from collapsing.

The great clock, made in 1380, has an inner and outer dial and shows the phases of the moon. At each quarter of an hour a tournament of knights takes place. The Bishop's Palace is separated from the cloisters by a moat and drawbridge.

Chalcot House (842488) near Westbury is a small Palladian style villa designed by the great Elizabethan architect, Robert Smythson. It contains a collection of modern paintings and Boer War memorabilia.

Longleat House (808430) was built by Sir John Thynne in 1580 and decorated in the Italian Renaissance style in the 19th century. It has fine libraries, state rooms, ceilings, pictures and furniture. The gardens were designed by Russell Page. There is a safari park containing hundreds of wild animals. There are many other tourist attractions with new additions each season.

Stourhead House (778342) was built in the 1720s and the gardens were laid out in the 1740s following a Grand Tour of Europe by the owner, Henry Hoare. The furniture includes some fine Chippendale and there are a number of paintings collected in Italy.

Tintinhull House (502198), built in the 17th century with a pedimental façade, is surrounded by superb modern formal gardens.

Lytes Cary Manor (533265) near Kingsdon has been the home of the Lyte family for 500 years. There is a 14th century chapel, a 15th century hall and a 16th century great chamber.

Nunney Castle
(Ref: 735459. Picture: I. Thompson)

Glastonbury Abbey (Ref: 5038. Picture: D. Pratt)

Wells Cathedral (Ref: 5545. Picture: D. Pratt)

The most important town on the map, in railway terms, is Yeovil (5516), which became the scene of a complex rail system and bitter rivalries, though there was no hint of any such battles when the first railways in the area were planned. To the north of this map is the Great Western Railway (GWR) main line from London to Bristol, opened in 1841. In 1845, the Wiltshire, Somerset and Weymouth Railway was formed to head south from that route to Salisbury, with a branch running off to Yeovil and on to Weymouth. At the same time, the Bristol and Exeter company, in effect an extension of the GWR main line, also planned a Yeovil branch. There were no real difficulties here, for both lines were planned to the same gauge as the GWR – Brunel's famous broad gauge, with rails set 7 ft apart, in contrast to the "standard" gauge, introduced first by George Stephenson, with rails 4 ft 8½ ins apart.

The Wiltshire, Somerset and Weymouth was, in fact, promoted by the GWR, but the progress was desperately slow. The line which appears at 866550 reached Westbury in 1848, at which point work came to a halt leaving bits of unconnected track over large areas of countryside. The independent company found it all too much, and the GWR stepped in. Soon there was an extension down to Warminster (8745) and from Frome through to the rich coalmining region centred on Radstock (6854). Locals tried to jolly the GWR along by promoting local companies, but it was the GWR who completed the route to Salis-

bury, leaving the map at 890451, and to Yeovil in 1856, with the extension down to Weymouth completed the following year. The GWR's own broad line reached Yeovil's outskirts in 1853 from the west, and joined the Wiltshire line the next year. It is now disused, and shows few traces on the map other than part of the triangular junction at 567158.

The GWR were not, however, the only party with their eyes on Yeovil. Their great rivals, the London and South Western Railway (LSWR) had their sights set on extending their standard gauge line westward to Exeter. In 1847 Parliament approved two Acts for lines that would reach the south west, one through the middle of the country, the other along the coast. But in spite of a costly Parliamentary battle, nothing very much actually happened and it

Cole Station in 1965

seemed as if the LSWR had lost interest in its grand designs – until Parliament itself prodded them into action. Work finally got under way on the Salisbury to Yeovil which was opened with an extension to Exeter in 1860. The GWR had a comparatively simple job with their route, but there was no way in which the LSWR could avoid expensive engineering as they cut through the hills and crossed the valleys. As the contours indicate this was a seesaw route, climbing out of Gillingham to the tunnel at Buckhorn Weston (7724) then down and up again to Templecombe (7022), followed immediately by a deep cutting on a steadily rising line before the descent to Yeovil. The citizens of Yeovil would have been better served by agreement than rivalries, with one station not two, though in this respect they were at least better off than the little cathedral town of Wells which was blessed, if that is the word, with three stations at one time – and now has none.

The railway system past and present

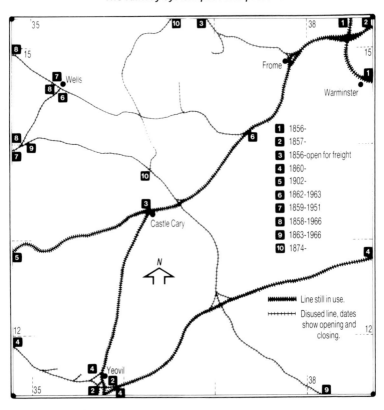

Witham, the junction of G.W.R. and East Somerset Railway, 1965
(Ref: 7440. Picture: Pamlin Prints)

The first line to appear was a GWR branch line from Glastonbury (5039), which opened in 1859. The East Somerset Railway ran from Witham (743407), initially only as far as Shepton Mallet, but extended to Wells in 1862. The western end through the hills has extensive cuttings and embankments, whereas the line to the east, though a little convoluted, has an easier passage and is still used for freight, by the quarries at 6944. In the middle at Cranmore (668430) is the East Somerset Railway Centre set up by the artist David Shepherd. It is home to a collection of steam locomotives, ranging from Black Prince, a British Rail Class 9F, one of the last great steam engines to be built in Britain, to a 1928 GWR tank engine. Trains are run over two miles of track, and

David Shepherd has a display of his work in the very appropriate setting of the old signal box.

The third line was the Cheddar Valley, the disused line running below the Mendips, and leaving the map at 490487.

The other major company to enter the field was the Somerset and Dorset Joint Railway. Although it is not shown on the map, there was once a line running west out of Glastonbury, the Somerset Central, linking the town to the Bristol Channel. The aim of the Somerset and Dorset was to use this as the first link in a chain that would take them across the country to the English Channel via the Dorset Central Railway. The line was originally built in parts, the Somerset company working down from their end to meet the Dorset men coming up toward them. The divided effort was not altogether satisfactory, but when they merged to form the Joint Company, work went ahead a good deal faster, and the route was completed in 1863. This is the disused line, running from 778150 to Glastonbury.

Encouraged by completion of the line, the company looked forward to days of prosperity, which were destined never to appear. They quickly ran into debt, and for a time locomotives could be seen bearing owners' name plates. They were creditors who allowed the company to run the locomotives more as an act of kindness than in any hope of recouping losses. The Somerset and Dorset decided that what they needed was more and more profitable traffic.

The Midland Railway opened a line between Bristol and Bath, and the Somerset and Dorset realised that an extension to that line would bring a new source of passengers and also tap into the Somerset coalfield market. This coalfield had first been served by the Somerset Coal Canal, which had been extended to Radstock by a tramway, an early form of railway in which horses not locomotives did the work. This was bought up and the line incorporated into the new route from Evercreech Junction (636371) to Bath, the disused line running up to Radstock. When the line opened in 1874 there was a vast increase in goods traffic, but not sufficient to restore the company's ailing finances.

Evercreech junction on the Somerset and Dorset joint railway, 1959

Wookey Hole (528479) is best known as a popular tourist attraction but it, too, was home to Neanderthal Man. The cave known as the Hyena Den yielded rich finds of stone axes and bones from cave lions, mammoths and woolly rhinos. It would seem to have been occupied alternately by man and hyenas in the last Ice Age. The first chamber was occupied right up to Roman times.

One of the country's most spectacular ancient sites is South Cadbury Castle (628252). The steep-sided hill is a natural defensive position which has been improved by earthworks. Ditches were dug round the hilltop, and the spoil piled up to form ramparts four and in places, five deep. There is a long history of settlement here, starting in Neolithic times around 3300 BC and continuing through the Bronze Age into the Iron Age. It was during the latter period, c. 500 BC that the great defensive system was begun, with the earthworks strengthened by stone blocks and timber palisades. A sizeable town was developed, but in AD 43 it was attacked and taken by the Roman

South Cadbury hill fort
(Ref: 6225. Picture: Cambridge University Collection of Air Photographs)

army under Vespasian and the inhabitants slaughtered. It remained in ruins until the 5th century AD, when it was again fortified and settled, with a great wooden hall in the centre. This was said to be Arthur's Camelot, and in legend Arthur and his Knights sleep under Cadbury Hill waiting for a fresh call to arms.

Other ancient sites are not nearly so impressive. In the area north of Priddy are four circles, centred on 540530, which were henges, built in Neolithic times around 2500 BC. These are simply earthworks with no standing stones and although they are impressive features on the map – and when seen from the air – they are difficult to spot on the ground. Around them are round barrows, Bronze Age burial mounds. There is another Iron Age hill fort at White Sheet Hill (803348), with an earlier Neolithic Camp just to the north. There is a complete, roughly oval earthwork, and it is assumed that the area was a gathering place where tribes met each year for rituals and ceremonials. Pen Pits (765318) are Iron Age quarries, where stone was dug for making querns, hand-operated grindstones for crushing grain into flour.

Ilchester began as the Roman town Lindinis. It was merely a fort when it was founded c. AD 50, but it developed as an inland port, with quays to the west of the present town. The Foss Way passes through the centre, and the line of the defensive walls can be seen to the west (525225).

Hillside, Sutton Montis, near Cadbury Castle (Ref: 6225)

Glastonbury Abbey (Ref: 5038)

The most famous early Christian site is Glastonbury Abbey (500388). It was almost certainly founded c. AD 700 by King Ini, but legend has associated it with various saints, notably St Joseph of Arimathea and it has been claimed as the burial place of King Arthur. The whole church was rebuilt at the end of the eleventh century, and again a century later following a fire. The present remains are very substantial, and are in a hybrid style, halfway between the massive simplicity of Norman architecture and the more elaborate gothic. The old abbot's kitchen is a well preserved square stone building with an octagonal roof and lantern, with a particularly good ribbed roof inside.

St Michael's Tower on the Tor marks a site of pre-Christian worship, which many believe still has special mystic significance. The fifteenth century abbey Courthouse or Tribunal in the High Street houses a museum, with remains from the Iron Age settlements in the levels, known as Lake villages. The other ruined abbey of note has fared far worse. Shaftesbury (862229) was a Benedictine nunnery in the ninth century and at the Dissolution most of the stone was taken away for building. All that remains is the excavated outline of the church., though finds from the site are on display in the attached museum.

The landscape of the countryside where the three counties of Somerset, Dorset and Wiltshire come together is attractive and varied, ranging from the limestone hills of the Mendips in the northwest, through a lower band of marls and clays, and rising again to chalk downlands in the east.

Ebbor Gorge (525485) is a dramatic ravine cut in the limestone of the Mendip edge near Wells by rivers which have now disappeared underground. Two nature trails allow exploration of the rich ash and oak woods: as well as the usual colourful woodland spring flowers, uncommon species such as nettle-leaved bellflower and greater butterfly orchid are to be found. A great variety of ferns also benefit from the damp, shady conditions – brittle bladderfern, Tunbridge filmy fern and maidenhair spleenwort are just some of the more unusual. Animal life is varied as well: badgers, sparrowhawks and the purple hairstreak butterfly are all present, and both greater and lesser horseshoe bats find a home in the cracks and crevices of the limestone rocks. The top of the gorge emerges into limestone heath and grassland, supporting a variety of butterflies, including the attractive marbled white.

The traditional importance of limestone in the local economy is indicated at Priddy Mineries (547515), an abandoned quarry. A nature reserve of the Somerset Trust for Nature Conservation, accessible along rights of way, the area has developed into limestone grassland, where adders may be seen basking, whilst the shallow pools which are present are home to a variety of dragonflies and damselflies, and to great crested newts. Stonechats are frequently seen in this area. Just to the east, there are walks through the Forestry Commission woodland of Stockhill (555510) where roe deer and woodland birds such as jays are to be seen.

Roe deer are also to be seen at Ammerdown Park (715535), where there is one of several nature trails in the area, running through coniferous and mixed deciduous woodland. Biddle Combe nature trail (569488)

The horseshoe bats are named because of the shape of their noses which are involved in echo-location. Bats are most often seen in the early evening in summer, as they leave their roosts in caves or trees to search for their food of insects.

Horses outside Chalcot House, Nr Westbury (Ref: 845488. Picture: I. Thompson)

follows the stream along a valley with both grassland and woodland habitats. The nature trail at Park Wood (559459) also passes through meadowland and damp woodland. Booklets for both these latter two are available from Wells Museum.

Just north east of Longleat (which, although best known for its safari park includes some magnificent old oak trees in its parkland, harbouring much native wildlife) is the National Trust-owned Cley Hill (839449). This dome-shaped chalk hill, with its Iron Age hill fort, supports a great diversity of chalkland flowers, including chalk milkwort, horseshoe vetch and a variety of orchids.

A much greater expanse of chalk downland is to be found on the National Trust estate of Fontmell Down (884184) which also takes in Melbury Beacon and Melbury Down. Much of Fontmell Down has never been ploughed or improved for agriculture, so that it retains a full complement of chalk-loving flowers, such as fairy flax, wild thyme, salad burnet, bee orchid and other orchids, as well as less common species such as early gentian and clustered bellflower. The flowers in turn attract a rich variety of butterflies. Although the downland is now protected, it cannot be neglected; the area is grazed with sheep in order to maintain the conditions of short turf which these chalkland flowers need in order to thrive.

INDUSTRIAL ARCHAEOLOGY

Frome was once an important centre of the West of England woollen trade. When Daniel Defoe came here in the early eighteenth century he wrote that "it is very likely to be one of the greatest and wealthiest inland towns in England." He also described the "many new streets of houses". Those houses, built for handloom weavers who worked at home, can still be seen off Trinity Street (772482). By the end of the century, work was moving into the new mills where first spinning, then weaving was carried on by mac-hines powered by water wheels. Many of these old mills can still be seen along the river, though none are now woollen mills. Adjoining chimneys show where steam power took over from water power in the nineteenth century. The last woollen cloth was produced in the town in 1965.

Shepton Mallet also had a busy woollen trade, though other textiles were also made. The former mill in Kilver Street (627436) was used for lace manufacture. Defoe, on his travels, described Glastonbury and Wells as centres for

Local roads' expert Gwyn Thomas investigates an overgrown green lane at Mendip

knitting stockings. The trade was so prosperous that weavers moved on to common land as squatters and built homes and workshops. Dilton Marsh (8449) is a typical, straggling squatters' village. Something of this story is told in local museums: the Wells Museum, Cathedral Green (552459), the Shepton Mallet Museum (618436) and the Somerset Rural Life Museum, Glastonbury (504385). The latter has a magnificent setting in the fourteenth century Abbey Barn.

The other major industry in the region was coal mining, centred on Radstock and Midsomer Norton. The last pit closed in 1973, leaving behind reminders in the shape of extensive spoil heaps and a few surface buildings around the towns. Another industry has survived, though in severely reduced form. The clear waters that emerge from Wookey Hole (522478) have been used for paper-making for two centuries. Of the several mills, one has been restored as a working museum of hand-paper-making. Two leats supply water for the turbines, which are still in situ. Only part of the mill is in use, and the rest of it is given over to very different activities. Here is a splendid collection of old fairground rides, including a steam galloper in full working order, with beautifully carved animals circling the puffing engine that provides the power. There are examples here of the work of the finest fairground animal carver, Arthur Anderson of Bristol. There is also an end-of-the-pier penny arcade of vintage slot machines, and Madame Tussaud's Cabinet of Curiosities, the story of the famous wax modeller. The principal attraction for visitors, however, is still the famous cave system, with its stalactites and stalagmites and underground river.

Somerset is famous for its agricultural produce. Cheddar cheese is now, it seems, made throughout the world, but the genuine, full-flavoured product is still turned out locally in the creamery at Chewton Mendip (5953). An appealing addition to the rural scene are the vineyards, two of which, Pilton (585406) and North Wootton (570423), are open to the public.

There are two specialist museums in the area: the Fleet Air Arm Museum at Yeovilton Airfield (5523) where there are more than 50 historic aircraft telling the story of the development of aviation at sea from 1908 to the present day. This is also the home of Concorde 002. There is a special flying viewing area. Coming back to earth, Sparkford is home to the Haynes Sparkford Motor Museum (608268), a collection of classic, veteran and vintage cars and motorcycles, all restored to full working order. Other less specialist, local history museums can be found at Castle Cary (641323), Shaftesbury (863228) and Yeovil (555157).

Local Information Centres

West Country Tourist Board
37 Southernhay East, Exeter
Devonshire EX1 1QS
(0392) 76351

Frome
Cattle Market Car Park
Somerset
(0373) 67271

Shepton Mallet
2 Petticoat Lane
Somerset BA4 5DA
(0749) 5258

Glastonbury
1 Marchant's Buildings
Northload Street
Somerset BA6 9JJ
(0458) 32954

Warminster
The Library, Three Horseshoes Mall
Wiltshire BA12 9BT
(0985) 218548

Wells
Town Hall, Market Place
Somerset BA5 2RB
(0749) 72552/75987

Automobile Association
Bristol Centre, Fanum House
26–32 Park Row
Bristol BS1 5LY
(0272) 290991

Travel

RAC road information
Bristol (0272) 732201
Rail information
Yeovil (0935) 21061
Bus information
Taunton (0823) 57533
Air information
Lulsgate (027 587) 4441

Nature Reserves

The Royal Society for Nature Conservation (0522-752326) provides contacts for local Wildlife Trusts who can advise on the best nature reserves to visit.

Touring Companions want you to enjoy the countryside without any problems for you, other visitors, or the people who must live and work there all year round. Please remember that there is no general right to wander in the countryside, although trespass is seldom a criminal offence. Stay on the rights of way marked on the Ordnance Survey map unless there is clear indication that access is permitted, or you have asked permission. Remember that not all disused railway lines are open to the public. Always obey the Country Code.

Enjoy the countryside and respect its life and work.
Guard against all risk of fire.
Fasten all gates.
Keep your dogs under close control.
Keep to public paths across farmland.
Use gates and stiles to cross fences, hedges and walls.
Leave livestock, crops and machinery alone.
Take your litter home.
Help to keep all water clean.
Protect wildlife, plants and trees.
Take special care on country roads.
Make no unnecessary noise.

National Grid references reproduced by permission of the Ordnance Survey, Southampton.

Bishops Palace and moat, Wells (Picture: D. Pratt)

Intricate detail of Wells Cathedral (Ref: 5595. Picture: D. Pratt)

Authors and artists in this volume include:

A. Burton, A. & A. Heaton, S. S. Kind, D. Young, E. Danielson, S. Qureshi, J. Slocombe, I. Thompson.